'I Absolve You'

Private Confession and the Church of England

Andrew Atherstone

The Latimer Trust

I am grateful to friends on the Group for the Renewal of Worship and the Latimer Theological Work Group for their comments on draft versions of this booklet.

Bible quotations are taken from the *New International Version*.

A.C.A.

'I Absolve You':
Private Confession and the Church of England

Published by the Latimer Trust
PO Box 26685
London N14 4XQ

www.latimertrust.org

CONTENTS

Chapter One:

Introduction

Reconciliation between sinful humanity and Almighty God is at the heart of the gospel message. The Christian church has good news to proclaim, that no matter how terrible our sins, forgiveness can be obtained through the sin-bearing death of Jesus Christ, the saviour of the world. When we repent of our wrongdoing and put our faith in Christ, we freely receive pardon and peace with God. The Apostle Paul explains that the church has been given 'the ministry of reconciliation: that God was reconciling the world to himself in Christ, not counting men's sins against them' (2 Corinthians 5.18-19).

Picking up Paul's phrase, the 'ministry of reconciliation' has become a shorthand way of describing the authoritative pronouncement of forgiveness for all who turn to Christ in penitence and faith. This ministry takes place in public (within the congregation, Sunday by Sunday) and also in private (with individuals, according to particular needs). The specific focus of this booklet is the 'ministry of reconciliation' with individuals – otherwise known as 'private confession' (or 'sacramental confession' or 'auricular confession'). Typically, a penitent recounts his sins in private to an ordained priest and then receives absolution, perhaps with the words 'I absolve you from all your sins'. Some Christians make use of private confession on special occasions – such as before Easter or when beginning a retreat. Others make it a frequent habit, perhaps every month or every week.

Many testify to the spiritual benefit of receiving this ministry. For example, in *Personal Confession Reconsidered,* Mark Morton writes of his discovery of private confession as 'a major turning point' in his Christian life. Beforehand he had a troubled conscience and was 'overwhelmed by feelings of unworthiness and inadequacy'. No amount of counsel took away these burdens. Only after private confession and priestly absolution was he able 'to look people in the eye and not to be overcome with guilt'.[1] Morton concludes that private confession is part of the church's 'treasure chest' and a vital means of spiritual growth.[2] Other authors, such as Gordon Oliver, speak of private confession as vital for pastoral care and a great missionary stimulus for the church.[3]

A contentious issue

Confession and absolution were hotly debated at the time of the Reformation and remain contentious issues today. Although the practice of private confession dropped out of the Church of England in the sixteenth century, it was revived by the Oxford Movement and its ritualist successors. J. H. Newman and E. B. Pusey began hearing confessions in 1838 and soon other clergy followed their example.[4] Between the 1840s and 1880s it was a matter of nationwide controversy. Private confession was thought by many to be a threat to the

---

[1] Mark Morton, *Personal Confession Reconsidered: Making Forgiveness Real,* Grove Spirituality Series no.50 (Nottingham: Grove Books, 1994), p 3.
[2] Ibid., p 18.
[3] Gordon Oliver, 'Guilt and Pastoral Care' in Trevor Lloyd and Phillip Tovey (eds.), *Celebrating Forgiveness: An Original Text Drafted by Michael Vasey,* Joint Liturgical Studies no.58 (Cambridge: Grove Books, 2004), p 39.
[4] Keith Denison, 'Dr Pusey as a Confessor and Spiritual Director' in Perry Butler (ed.), *Pusey Rediscovered* (London: SPCK, 1983), pp 210-230.

integrity of the Victorian family. This idea was reinforced by a number of scandals involving young clergymen asking married women to confess the details of their sexual desires. More significantly, private confession was also thought to be unbiblical and a betrayal of Reformation principles. Ritualist clergy were condemned as 'Jesuits in disguise'.[5]

One leading Victorian evangelical, Bishop J. C. Ryle, spoke for many when he declared that he would rather his children were dead than that they went to confession:

> 'Once more I repeat my warning. No priest but Christ! No confessor but Christ! No absolver but Christ! No habitual private submission or bowing down in religion to anyone but Christ! No spiritual director but Christ! No putting of our conscience in the power of anyone but Christ! If we love peace and wish to honour Christ, let us beware of the confessional, or the slightest approach to it. I declare I had almost rather hear my sons and daughters had gone to the grave, than hear they had adopted the habit of going to a confessional.' [6]

While bishops like Ryle fought against private confession from pulpit and pamphlet, others fought against it with their fists. Protestant agitators such as John Kensit and his Wickliffe Preachers roamed the country disrupting ritualist services. Their slogan was uncompromising: 'No priest but Christ, no sacrifice but Calvary, no confessional but the throne of grace, no authority but the Word of God.' Echoes of these tensions have continued to rumble on within the

---

[5] Nigel Yates, '"Jesuits in Disguise"? Ritualist Confessors and their Critics in the 1870s', *Journal of Ecclesiastical History* 39 (April 1988), pp 202-216. See further, Nigel Yates, *Anglican Ritualism in Victorian Britain, 1830-1910* (Oxford: OUP, 1999); J. S. Reed, *Glorious Battle: The Cultural Politics of Victorian Anglo-Catholicism* (London: Tufton, 1998); John Kent, *Holding the Fort: Studies in Victorian Revivalism* (London: Epworth, 1978), ch 7.
[6] J. C. Ryle, *Knots Untied* (1874; republished Moscow, Idaho: Charles Nolan, 2000), p 272.

Church of England. As recently as 1983 a modern language rite for 'The Reconciliation of a Penitent' failed to secure a majority in the House of Laity at General Synod, because of evangelical objections to the words 'I absolve you'.[7]

A new theological climate

The theological climate is now considerably altered compared to a hundred, or even fifty, years ago. Both Pusey and Ryle would be amazed if they were to return to the Church of England today. Private confession is no longer a 'party' issue, with clear lines dividing separate theological camps. Since the 1960s there has been a growing cross-fertilization between different viewpoints. Private confession is now increasingly welcomed and practised across a wide theological spectrum.

Within the Roman Catholic and Anglo-Catholic movements the situation has changed dramatically in recent decades. Long queues to the confessional box during Holy Week, once common, have vanished. Indeed the confessional box itself – where priest and penitent met in anonymity separated by a screen – has all but disappeared. There is a new emphasis on flexibility, informality and face-to-face contact. Following the Second Vatican Council, the Roman Church produced a revised liturgy of reconciliation, *Ordo Penitentiae* (1973). Although bound by the dogmatic parameters of the Council of Trent, this new rite has a less medieval 'feel'. Private confession today is conducted much like a pastoral interview, tailored according to individual needs.

---

[7] General Synod, *Report of Proceedings* vol.14 (February 1983), pp 47-75.

Within the evangelical movement things have also changed dramatically in recent decades. There is a growing interest amongst evangelicals in 'catholic' spirituality – such as spiritual direction, Ignatian prayer, retreats and pilgrimages. Many are now open to the idea of private confession as a part of spiritual growth. For example, David Watson, a leading evangelical charismatic, recommended that all Christians regularly confess their sins to a friend or to a 'counsellor'. He saw this as necessary for healthy church life.[8] Similar advice is given by Neil T. Anderson (President of Freedom in Christ Ministries), one of the most popular evangelical authors on spiritual warfare and exorcism. His best-selling book, *The Bondage Breaker*, suggests that we ask our 'pastor or Christian counsellor' to lead us through the seven 'steps to freedom', which involve a detailed confession of sin.[9]

Within this new and conciliatory theological climate, the Church of England has produced its own rite for 'The Reconciliation of a Penitent', as part of the liturgical provision of *Common Worship*. Other provinces around the Anglican Communion have used such prayers for decades (beginning with the Church of the Province of South Africa in 1954) and the Church of England is following suit. This booklet aims to look afresh at the principles behind private confession and priestly absolution. Three vital questions need to be asked of this practice: 'Is it biblical?', 'Is it Anglican?' and 'Is it helpful?' We begin, by way of setting the scene, with some important history.

---

[8] David Watson, *Discipleship* (London: Hodder & Stoughton, 1981), pp 52-54.
[9] Neil Anderson, *The Bondage Breaker* (new edition, London: Monarch, 2000), chs 13-14.

Chapter Two:

Scholastics versus Reformers

The 'ministry of reconciliation' is the new name for what used to be called the 'sacrament of penance'. The origins of penance remain obscure, lost in the mists of time. In the early church penance was public rather than private, part of the discipline of notorious sinners. Those who had been excommunicated for serious crimes were publicly reconciled to the church, usually at the end of Lent. Public penance was gradually superseded by private penance, which first began to appear in the West in the middle of the fifth century. The New Testament word *metanoia* ('repentance') was translated in the Latin Vulgate as *poenitentia*, which came to be understood as 'penance'. One early English translation of the Bible (Douay-Rheims) had John the Baptist exhorting the crowds: 'Do penance, for the kingdom of heaven is at hand'.[10]

The Middle Ages

By the Middle Ages, penance had evolved into an elaborate theological system and was elevated into the role of a 'sacrament'. Scholastic theologians, such as Peter Abelard, Hugh of St Victor, Peter Lombard and Thomas Aquinas, debated its precise details. At the fourth Lateran Council in

---

[10] For the history of penance, see R. C. Mortimer, *The Origins of Private Penance in the Western Church* (Oxford: Clarendon Press, 1939); Paul Palmer, *Sacraments and Forgiveness* (London: DLT, 1960); Thomas Tentler, *Sin and Confession on the Eve of the Reformation* (Princeton NJ: Princeton University Press, 1977); James Dallen, *The Reconciling Community* (New York: Pueblo, 1986).

1215, private penance was made compulsory for every Christian at least once a year. Those who did not comply were to be excommunicated and refused a Christian burial.[11] According to the scholastics, the 'sacrament of penance' had three constituent parts:

- *contrition* (of heart) – sorrow for having sinned and a determination not to sin again. The medieval theologians also developed the idea of *attrition*, an imperfect form of contrition. While contrition arises from love of God, attrition arises from servile fear of God.

- *confession* (of mouth) – a spoken avowal to a priest of every sin one remembers.

- *satisfaction* (of works) – acts of reparation decreed by the priest, such as fasting, prayer, almsgiving and going on pilgrimage.

When these three parts of the 'sacrament of penance' were satisfactorily completed, they were followed by

- *absolution* – forgiveness pronounced by the priest, usually with the words *'Ego te absolvo a peccatis tuis'* (I absolve you of your sins).

Medieval theologians argued about which parts of penance were essential and which optional. The doctrine reached its culmination in Thomas Aquinas, who insisted upon all four elements. He taught that no one who sins after baptism can be reconciled to God without the priest's absolution, using the *'Ego te absolvo'* formula.[12] Other schoolmen disagreed, such as Duns Scotus and William of Ockham, but it was the

---

[11] Fourth Lateran Council (1215), constitution 21. See Norman Tanner (ed.), *Decrees of the Ecumenical Councils* [COD] (London: Sheed & Ward, 1990), p 245.
[12] Thomas Aquinas, *Summa Theologica*, part 3, questions 84-90.

Thomist view which swept the board. Aquinas' dogma was taken up by the Council of Florence in 1439 and remains the official teaching of the Roman Church today.[13] In the sixteenth century the Council of Trent went further and made the sacrament of penance (including regular private confession) a condition of going to Mass. The Council anathematised those who denied either its divine origin or its necessity for salvation.[14]

The Reformation

The Roman penitential system came under sustained theological attack during the Reformation and was ultimately abolished in Reformation churches. The Reformers were not only critical of the abuses of the confessional, such as the immorality and ignorance of many confessors and the sale of 'indulgences' (giving money to Vatican coffers in lieu of satisfaction for sins). They were also critical of its underlying theological principles. They sternly denied that private confession is either of divine origin or necessary for salvation. Moreover, the Reformers saw it as undermining the gospel by encouraging penitents to earn forgiveness from God through good works and human merit, rather than through the merits of Christ alone appropriated by faith alone. They viewed private confession and priestly absolution as a tyrannical enslavement to human mediators, which obscures the work of Christ, our great high priest.

---

[13] Council of Florence, session 8, 22 November 1439 (Bull of union with the Armenians); COD, p 548.
[14] Council of Trent, sessions 13 & 14, 11 October 1551 & 25 November 1551; COD, pp 696, 698, 703-713.

One of the first to challenge the system of private confession was John Wycliffe, the 'morning star of the Reformation'. He insisted that compulsory confession to a priest is without biblical warrant, although he commended it as useful if entered into voluntarily. Martin Luther assailed the practice, although he still occasionally described penance as a 'sacrament'.[15] John Calvin went further, rejecting private confession outright as 'useless and fruitless ... utterly worthless ... utterly false', a custom which should be 'banished from our midst – a thing so pestilent and in so many ways harmful to the church!'[16] In England, during the early days of the Reformation in the 1530s, private confession was maintained as a regular practice. By the 1550s, as the Reformation got into full swing, it was abolished.

Many of the Reformers were happy to maintain the old medieval names, such as 'penance', 'satisfaction' and 'absolution'. However, they understood these concepts in a radically different way to their Roman contemporaries.

Contrition. The Reformers agreed that contrition is a biblical idea (e.g. Psalm 51.17, Luke 18.13, Acts 2.37, 2 Corinthians 7.10). Yet whereas the scholastics demanded that penitents be 'fully' or 'duly' contrite, the Reformers insisted that this is impossible. Our contrition is always imperfect and instead of desperately trying to stir up sufficient remorse we should focus instead upon the Lord's mercy.

Confession. The Reformers agreed that confession of sin is a vital part of Christian life, but that this should be to God

---

[15] David Bagchi, 'Luther and the Sacramentality of Penance' in Kate Cooper and Jeremy Gregory (eds.), *Retribution, Repentance, and Reconciliation* (Woodbridge: Boydell Press, 2004), pp 119-127.
[16] John Calvin, *Institutes of the Christian Religion* (1559), III. iv. 19.

directly rather than to a human priest. The scholastics demanded a 'full' confession, but again the Reformers insisted that this is impossible. Our sins are so many that we cannot even begin to number them (e.g. Psalm 19.12). As Calvin colourfully put it, 'how deep is the pit of our sins, how many are the faces of crime, how many heads this hydra bore, and what a long tail it dragged along.'[17]

Satisfaction. The Reformers refuted the scholastic claim that we can earn God's forgiveness or pay our debts to God by good works, such as fasting and almsgiving. Christ alone made satisfaction to God for sin, through his death on the cross once for all. As the *Book of Common Prayer* proclaims, Christ 'made there (by his one oblation of himself once offered) a full, perfect, and sufficient sacrifice, oblation, and satisfaction, for the sins of the whole world ...' We are justified by grace alone through faith alone in Christ alone. The gift of forgiveness is totally free (e.g. Romans 3.24, Ephesians 2.8, 2 Timothy 1.9, Titus 3.5).

While it is impossible to make any satisfaction to God, the Reformers agreed that it is essential to make satisfaction to the people against whom we have sinned. We must make amends, where possible, by restoring relationships, returning stolen goods and contradicting our former lies. Such restitution is demanded and commended in the Bible (e.g. Leviticus 6.1-5, Numbers 5.5-7, Luke 19.8, 2 Corinthians 7.11).

Absolution. The Reformers taught that no one can forgive sins, except God alone. The forgiveness of God does not depend upon the judgment of human beings. Christ alone is our absolver. Forgiveness of sins is not only guaranteed by

---

[17] Ibid., III. iv. 16.

his death on the cross, but also administered by him. The Reformers understood ministerial absolution as a *declaration* or *pronouncement* of God's forgiveness for all who repent and put their faith in Christ Jesus. They maintained that this authority lay not in the priesthood but in the gospel, not in the words of men but in the Word of God. Ministerial absolution is thus a reminder of the Bible's promises about God's terms for forgiveness.

Culpa and Poena

The scholastics made their penitential system even more complicated by distinguishing between the *culpa* (guilt) of sin and the *poena* (penalty / punishment) of sin. *Poena* was further divided into *poena aeterna* (eternal punishment) and *poena temporalis* (temporal punishment). They taught that the satisfaction of Christ is sufficient to free the contrite sinner from *culpa* but not *poena*. Only penance can remove *poena aeterna,* while the fires of purgatory (for all but the holiest saints) are needed to remove *poena temporalis.*

In contrast, the Reformers insisted that Christ's death brings freedom from all sin and all the consequences of sin, to those who repent and believe the gospel. God forgives *fully* as well as *freely.* They taught that the trials of life which come to believers are not a punishment for sin or the means of satisfying God. Rather they are the loving chastisements of a Heavenly Father, to deepen repentance, strengthen faith and increase holiness.

Chapter Three:

Is it Biblical?

Confession of our sins is one of the key aspects of the Christian life and is crucial for our spiritual vitality. As wise King Solomon puts it: 'He who conceals his sins does not prosper, but whoever confesses and renounces them finds mercy' (Proverbs 28.13). In the Bible, three types of confession are taught:

i.) Confession to God

Every sin is a rebellion against God, when we break his laws and fall short of his demands. Although many of our sins are committed against other people, they are primarily sins against God and so must be confessed first and foremost to him. This type of confession is essential (e.g. Psalm 32, Psalm 51, 1 John 1.8-9). It must be habitual, immediate and thorough. Penitents in the Bible confess their sins directly to God in secret and also, on occasion, corporately as part of a congregation (e.g. 1 Samuel 7.2-6, Nehemiah 9, Ezra 9.1-10.1).

ii.) Confession to our Neighbour

Our sins often bring sorrow and suffering to other people. The Bible instructs us to seek reconciliation with anyone we have wronged, making reparation where possible for the harm we have caused. This may involve confessing a particular sin to the person sinned against and asking for forgiveness from them (e.g. Matthew 5.23-24, James 5.16).

'Sorry' is one of the hardest words to say, but one of the most liberating. There is nothing official or 'liturgical' about this type of confession. Rather it is a natural and *ad hoc* part of Christian friendship.

iii.) Confession to the Congregation

Flagrant sins harm the whole Christian community, as seen in the case of Achan (Joshua 7) and the sexual immorality at Corinth (1 Corinthians 5). Public sins sometimes require public church discipline, such as excommunication. As part of their restoration to Christian fellowship, notorious sinners may need to confess their sin publicly to the congregation as a witness to repentance and to seek forgiveness from the congregation for the damage done.

These three types of confession are all seen in the Bible, with overwhelming emphasis upon the first. As John Stott observes, the general principle is that confession is due to the one against whom we have sinned and from whom we need forgiveness.[18] Therefore confession is always due to God and is sometimes due to people as well.

However, there is no trace in the Bible of any other type of confession. Nothing can be found, even by hint or implication, referring to private confession. Private confession is, by definition, not made to the one sinned against, but to a priest. It is called 'auricular' for good reason – that is, confession *ad auriculam* ('into the ear' of the priest), what the Reformers nicknamed 'earish' confession. Nor is there any trace in the Bible of priestly absolution – that is, of

---

[18] John Stott, *Confess Your Sins: The Way of Reconciliation* (London: Hodder & Stoughton, 1964), p 12. This booklet owes much to John Stott's excellent book.

ordained ministers being given the authority literally to forgive or absolve sins on God's behalf.

Some Disputed Texts

Advocates of private confession and priestly absolution offer various proof texts to show that it is taught in the New Testament. We will examine each in turn.

Mark 1.44 and parallels

When Jesus met a man suffering from leprosy (a disease linked in the Bible with spiritual uncleanness), he instructed him to 'go, show yourself to the priest'. Some suggest, therefore, that when we sin we must resort to an ordained priest to receive spiritual healing and forgiveness.

It is clear from the Old Testament, however, that the priests of Israel had no power, and could offer no ritual, to heal disease. Healing was left entirely in the hands of God. It is Jesus who heals the leper with the command 'Be clean!', and the disease leaves 'immediately' (Mark 1.42). The role of the priest is merely to certify the cure so that the man can retake his place in Jewish society (Leviticus 13-14) and as 'a testimony' to the healing power of Jesus. There is no hint here of the modern practice of private confession and priestly absolution.

Mark 2.10 and parallels

When Jesus healed a paralysed man in Capernaum, he declared that 'the Son of Man has authority on earth to forgive sins'. Some suggest that by using the title 'Son of Man' Jesus is emphasising his humanity. Therefore, the argument goes, his authority to forgive sins is not based on his divinity but on the authority which the Father has given him as representative and head of the human race. Indeed the crowd praised God 'who had given such authority *to men*' (Matthew 9.8). So, by implication, other human beings also have the authority to forgive sins.

It is far from clear that the title 'Son of Man' is a reference to Jesus' humanity. This title is also used throughout the Gospels to indicate his divine origin and as a way of expressing his relationship to God. When he healed the paralysed man, Jesus made no attempt to challenge the statement by the teachers of the law, 'Who can forgive sins but God alone?' (Mark 2.7). In fact, his pronouncement of the man's forgiveness is intended as a declaration of his own divinity.

Mark 1.5 / Acts 19.18

When John the Baptist exhorted the Judean crowds to 'Repent, for the kingdom of heaven is near', they responded by confessing their sins before being baptised in the River Jordan (Matthew 3.1-6, Mark 1.4-5). Likewise, during Paul's mission to Ephesus, many of the new believers openly confessed their evil practices (Acts 19.17-20).

There is no hint here of private confession or priestly absolution. In neither case are we told to whom confession was made, and probably it was in public. Nor are these confessions a recital of all known sins – indeed, in the case of John the Baptist's converts they may have been 'general' rather than specific. What is recorded here is not a habitual practice, but a one-off event – a drastic renunciation of the past, at the time of conversion. Many movements of the Holy

Spirit down the centuries have been characterised by this sort of informal public confession.

James 5.16

> 'Is any one of you sick? He should call the elders of the church to pray over him and anoint him with oil in the name of the Lord. And the prayer offered in faith will make the sick person well; the Lord will raise him up. If he has sinned, he will be forgiven. Therefore confess your sins to each other and pray for each other so that you may be healed. The prayer of a righteous man is powerful and effective.' (James 5.14-16)

This passage implies that church leaders have a specific role in praying for the sick, but says nothing about hearing confessions. Despite the choice of 'priests' rather than 'elders' in the Rheims New Testament of 1582, there is no hint of priestly absolution. Indeed if private confession was meant, then the priest would also have to confess to the penitent, since this is reciprocal ('to each other'). James' command may refer to mutual confession of sins within the Christian community, in a spirit of openness and honesty – as witnessed amongst the early Methodists or in the East African Revival. Or it may refer to those who have offended each other making their peace together.

2 Corinthians 2.10

Paul tells the Corinthians: 'If you forgive anyone, I also forgive him. And what I have forgiven – if there was anything to forgive – I have forgiven in the sight of Christ for your sake, in order that Satan might not outwit us.' (2 Corinthians 2.10-11)

Once again, this verse has nothing to do with private confession or priestly absolution. Paul is referring to someone who has sinned against the apostle and the Christian congregation in Corinth and has caused them 'grief' (v.5). The sinner has been punished, probably by excommunication (v.6). Paul now urges the believers to forgive the banished brother and 'reaffirm your love for him' (vv.7-8). They have authority to forgive such sins against the church, but not sins against God.

Matthew 16.19 and 18.18

After Simon Peter's declaration at Caesarea Philippi that Jesus is 'the Christ, the Son of the living God', Jesus replied:

> 'Blessed are you, Simon son of Jonah, for this was not revealed to you by man, but by my Father in heaven. And I tell you that you are Peter, and on this rock I will build my church, and the gates of Hades will not overcome it. I will give you the keys of the kingdom of heaven; whatever you bind on earth will be bound in heaven, and whatever you loose on earth will be loosed in heaven.' (Matthew 16.17-19)

Later, speaking to the disciples generally, Jesus said:

> 'If your brother sins against you, go and show him his fault, just between the two of you. If he listens to you, you have won your brother over. But if he will not listen, take one or two others along, so that "every matter may be established by the testimony of two or three witnesses." If he refuses to listen to them, tell it to the church; and if he refuses to listen even to the church, treat him as you would a pagan or a tax collector. I tell you the truth, whatever you bind on earth will be bound in heaven, and whatever you loose on earth will be loosed in heaven.' (Matthew 18.15-18)

These two texts are often offered as proof of the doctrine of priestly absolution, but they contain no such idea. Rather they are about the preaching of the gospel and the exercise of church discipline.

In rabbinic literature, to 'bind' and 'loose' are often used to mean to 'forbid' and 'allow'. They also refer to imposing and lifting a ban of excommunication from the synagogue. In other words, Peter and the local church are given authority by Christ to decide (under the guidance of the Holy Spirit and in accordance with the Scriptures) what actions are allowed or forbidden within the Christian community. Some forms of behaviour will be welcomed, others will lead to excommunication. This interpretation is supported by the wider context of Matthew 18 and the fact that Jesus is talking about binding and loosing things not people ('*whatever* you bind' not '*whoever* you bind'). We see such 'binding' and 'loosing' in action at the Jerusalem Council in Acts 15.

Closely linked with this exercise of church discipline is authority to preach the gospel – which is what Jesus means when he gives Peter 'the keys of the kingdom'. The Pharisees and teachers of the law had 'shut the kingdom of heaven in men's faces' (Matthew 23.13) and Peter was to use the keys to open it. According to this figure of speech, the kingdom of heaven is 'opened' and 'shut' when the gospel is proclaimed. It is 'opened' when hearers are told that their sins will be forgiven if they repent and put their faith in Christ. It is 'closed' when hearers are told that their sins will remain unforgiven if they reject Christ and refuse to repent. Peter was the first to use 'the keys of the kingdom' because he had the unique privilege of being the first person to preach the good news to both Jews (Acts 2) and Gentiles (Acts 10).

On the first evening after the Resurrection, Jesus appeared to his disciples, who were hiding behind locked doors 'for fear of the Jews'. The Apostle John recalls:

> 'Jesus said, "Peace be with you! As the Father has sent me, I am sending you." And with that he breathed on them and said, "Receive the Holy Spirit. If you forgive anyone his sins, they are forgiven; if you do not forgive them, they are not forgiven."' (John 20.21-23)

Older translations speak here of 'remitting' and 'retaining' sins, and this verse has again been used as support for the doctrine of priestly absolution.

It is important to note, firstly, that this promise is not given exclusively to the apostles but indiscriminately to the whole church. There were other disciples there besides the Eleven (see Luke 24.33-36). Indeed on this occasion it was only the Ten, because Thomas was absent – and surely he is given the same authority as the rest! Moreover, the pouring out of the Holy Spirit, which Jesus demonstrates in an acted parable by breathing out upon them, was not restricted to the apostles but bestowed upon every Christian. The authority to 'remit' and 'retain' sins is distributed equally widely.

This pair of statements (to remit and retain) is parallel to the two pairs we have already examined in Matthew's Gospel (to bind and loose; to open and shut). It has the same meaning. To 'remit' and 'retain' sins is to proclaim the Christian gospel. This passage is parallel to the Great Commission in Luke 24.46-49 – both refer to the evangelisation of the world, the gift of the Holy Spirit and the offer of forgiveness. In Luke's Gospel the disciples are told to preach 'repentance and forgiveness of sins' in the name of

Jesus to all nations. In John's Gospel, the 'remission' and 'retention' of sins is the substance of that message.

Admittedly this is a dramatic figure of speech (like 'hating' our parents, or 'plucking out' our eye, or 'taking up our cross', or 'losing our life'.) In the Old Testament, Jeremiah is told that he is appointed over nations 'to destroy and overthrow, to build and to plant' (Jeremiah 1.10). This is a reference to Jeremiah's ministry of preaching and prophecy – his declaration of the judgment and salvation of God. In the same way, in the New Testament, Christians are given authority to 'retain' and 'remit' sins. This is a reference to our ministry of preaching and proclamation, the warning of judgment to the unbeliever and the promise of salvation to the believer.

The Acts of the Apostles

The first Christians never spoke or behaved as if they had been given authority to forgive sins. They never claimed such power or attempted to exercise it. They never heard confessions or offered priestly absolution. Instead the first Christians preached the gospel and exercised church discipline. They spoke of God's grace and God's judgment. They proclaimed God's terms for forgiving sins (repentance and faith in Christ) and then admitted penitent believers by baptism into the church. This is what we see throughout the Book of Acts:

> 'Repent and be baptised, every one of you, in the name of Jesus Christ for the forgiveness of your sins.' (Acts 2.38)

> 'Repent, then, and turn to God, so that your sins may be wiped out ...' (Acts 3.19)

'All the prophets testify about him that everyone who believes in him receives forgiveness of sins through his name.' (Acts 10.43)

'Therefore, my brothers, I want you to know that through Jesus the forgiveness of sins is proclaimed to you.' (Acts 13.38)

The Epistles

In the New Testament epistles the picture is the same. There is nothing, even in the later Pastorals, alluding to private confession and priestly absolution. There is much about the exercise of church discipline (e.g. 1 Corinthians 5.1-5, 2 Corinthians 2.5-11, 2 Thessalonians 3.14-15, 1 Timothy 1.20, Titus 3.9-11). This was open and public discipline, in the hope of the sinner's eventual restoration to Christian fellowship. There is also much in the epistles proclaiming the gospel. We read triumphant affirmations that 'in Christ we have redemption through his blood, the forgiveness of sins' (Ephesians 1.7, cf. Colossians 1.14). And that 'Christ died for sins once for all, the righteous for the unrighteous, to bring you to God' (1 Peter 3.18). And that Christ 'is the atoning sacrifice for our sins, and not only for ours but also for the sins of the whole world' (1 John 2.2).

This is the message, from beginning to end, of the New Testament. This was the message of the early Christians. This is how Paul understood the 'ministry of reconciliation' – not as a 'sacrament of penance' or a rite of private confession and priestly absolution, but as a heartfelt appeal for men and women to be reconciled to God through Christ. All Christians are Christ's ambassadors, commissioned to implore others on Christ's behalf: 'Be reconciled to God ... now is the time of God's favour, now is the day of salvation' (2 Corinthians 5.18 – 6.2).

Chapter Four:

Is it Anglican?

Is private confession a traditional Anglican practice? Is it permitted by the formularies of the Church of England? What are we to make of the scattered references to confession and absolution in the *Book of Common Prayer*? [19]

The Reformation in England took place by degrees. The old scholastic teaching about penance was only slowly dismantled. In the reign of Henry VIII a number of official declarations in the 1530s and 40s spoke of penance as a 'sacrament' and private confession as 'expedient and necessary'. [20] Yet when the Reformers were given a free hand in the reign of Edward VI from 1547, the situation began to change more rapidly. It is not true that they merely made optional what was compulsory in the Roman church. In fact they challenged the very principles on which the Roman

---

[19] See especially, T. W. Drury, *Confession and Absolution: The Teaching of the Church of England, as Interpreted and Illustrated by the Writings of the Reformers of the Sixteenth Century* (London: Hodder & Stoughton, 1903).

[20] During the 1530s and 40s there was a theological tug-of-war between Reformers and conservatives, as seen in contrasting doctrinal statements. Article III of the Ten Articles (1536) describes the sacrament of penance as 'necessary for man's salvation'; Article VIII of Cranmer's unofficial Thirteen Articles (1538) calls auricular confession 'very useful and highly necessary'; the Act of Six Articles (1539) calls auricular confession 'expedient and necessary to be retained and continued, used and frequented, in the Church of God'. Meanwhile the Bishop's Book (1537) put a pro-Protestant interpretation upon the Ten Articles, but the reactionary King's Book (1543) described the sacrament of penance as 'the ordinary mean for penitent sinners to obtain remission of sins'. These articles can be found in Gerald Bray (ed.), *Documents of the English Reformation* (second edition, Cambridge: James Clarke, 2004).

system was built. In the reformed Church of England, the entire centre of gravity of the penitential system shifted. Where habitual private confession to a priest had been the norm, habitual confession directly to Almighty God became the norm. The usual pattern was now self-examination, followed by 'general' confession and absolution during public worship – the absolution taking declaratory form ('Almighty God forgives ...') or precatory form ('May Almighty God forgive ...').[21] Although private confession was not completely outlawed, it was only for use in abnormal circumstances as a means of relieving a troubled conscience. This is the emphasis found in Cranmer's Prayer Book of 1552 and maintained by the Caroline revisers in 1662. We will examine the relevant parts of this liturgical provision in turn.

Morning and Evening Prayer

Morning and Evening Prayer begin with an explanation that 'although we ought at all times humbly to acknowledge our sins before God; yet ought we most chiefly so to do, when we assemble and meet together ...'. This is Cranmer's gentle attempt to remind us that confession should be made directly to Almighty God, not to a priest; and that it should be made corporately within the congregation, not in the privacy of a priest's booth. It is followed immediately by a 'general' confession. Instead of the formula *Ego te absolvo*, the absolution is a declaration that God 'pardoneth and absolveth all them that truly repent, and unfeignedly believe his holy

---

[21] See further, Andrew Atherstone, *'Search Me, O God': The Practice of Self-Examination*, Grove Spirituality Series no.87 (Cambridge: Grove Books, 2003); Andrew Atherstone, *Confessing Our Sins*, Grove Worship Series no.179 (Cambridge: Grove Books, 2004).

Gospel'. Sadly this declaratory form of absolution has almost died out in the Church of England and is totally absent from *Common Worship*.

Holy Communion

In the medieval church, the usual way to prepare for Mass was by private confession. In the reformed church, the usual way to prepare for the Lord's Supper was by 'general' confession in the congregation. As the Reformation progressed, these two perspectives overlapped for a while. The Prayer Book of 1549 urged people to follow their own conscience and live in peace with those of opposing views. Yet by 1552 private confession had been swept away. The contrast is important as illustrating the intentions of the Reformers.

The 1549 Prayer Book exhorts us:

'And if there be any of you whose conscience is troubled and grieved in anything, lacking comfort or counsel, let him come to me, or to some other discreet and learned priest taught in the law of God, and confess and open his sin and grief secretly, that he may receive such ghostly counsel, advice, and comfort, that his conscience may be relieved, and that of us (as of the ministers of God and of the church) he may receive comfort and absolution, to the satisfaction of his mind and the avoiding of all scruple and doubtfulness. Requiring such as shall be satisfied with a general confession, not to be offended with them that do use, to their further satisfying, the auricular and secret confession to the priest. Nor those also which think needful or convenient for the quietness of their own consciences particularly to open their sins to the priest, to be offended with them that are satisfied with their humble confession to God and the general confession to the church. But in all things to follow and keep the rule of charity, and every man to be satisfied with his own conscience, not judging other men's minds or consciences; whereas he hath no warrant of God's word to the same.'

Yet now the 1662 Prayer Book exhorts us (with substantially the same words as 1552):

'And because it is requisite, that no man should come to the holy Communion, but with a full trust in God's mercy, and with a quiet conscience; therefore if there be any of you, who by this means [self-examination, confession to God, reconciliation with neighbours] cannot quiet his own conscience herein, but requireth further comfort or counsel, let him come to me, or to some other discreet and learned Minister of God's Word, and open his grief; that by the ministry of God's holy Word he may receive the benefit of absolution, together with ghostly counsel and advice, to the quieting of his conscience, and avoiding of all scruple and doubtfulness.'

There are a number of significant changes between these two exhortations which are worthy of note:

- Private confession is now clearly meant to be an exception rather than the rule, for use only in rare circumstances.

- The troubled person is to 'open his grief' not 'confess his sin'. In other words, this is not an enumeration of all the penitent's sins, but of the particular issue which worries him. As Henry Bullinger observes, it would best be called a 'consultation' rather than a 'confession'.[22]

- The troubled person is to go to a 'Minister of God's Word' not to a 'priest'. Although this may be the local clergyman, it may equally be a wise and biblically literate layperson. In 1662 some wanted the word 'priest' reinstated, but this proposal was rejected.

---

[22] Henry Bullinger, 'Of Repentance and the Causes Thereof', *The Decades* IV (Cambridge: Parker Society, 1851), p 75.

- The troubled person is to receive comfort and absolution not from the minister himself, but from the ministry of the Word. As R. B. Girdlestone (first Principal of Wycliffe Hall, Oxford) succinctly put it: 'whilst the enquirer opens his grief the minister opens his Bible'.[23] The minister is to apply the Bible to the particular need, which will include offering spiritual counsel and advice. He will point the penitent to passages in Scripture which clearly explain how we are reconciled to God through repentance and faith in Christ. The authoritative message of assurance comes not from the words of the minister, but from the Word of God.

Later in the Holy Communion service, we see these principles in action. Instead of the formula *'Ego te absolvo'*, the absolution is a prayer for God to forgive those who turn to him 'with hearty repentance and true faith'. This is immediately followed by some 'comfortable words' from Scripture which remind us about the work of Jesus Christ on which our forgiveness is based:

'Come unto me all that travail and are heavy laden, and I will refresh you.' (Matthew 11.28)

'So God loved the world, that he gave his only-begotten Son, to the end that all that believe in him should not perish, but have everlasting life.' (John 3.16)

'This is a true saying, and worthy of all men to be received, that Christ Jesus came into the world to save sinners.' (1 Timothy 1.15)

---

[23] R. B. Girdlestone, H. C. G. Moule and T. W. Drury, *English Church Teaching on Faith, Life and Order* (London: Charles Murray, 1898), p 50. For Girdlestone's view of the Bible, see Andrew Atherstone, 'Robert Baker Girdlestone and "God's Own Book"', *Evangelical Quarterly* 74 (October 2002), pp 313-332.

'If any man sin, we have an Advocate with the Father, Jesus Christ the righteous, and he is the propitiation for our sins.' (1 John 2.1-2)

Thus the penitent believer is sent home assured of pardon, with these Bible promises ringing in his ears. Sadly, of the fifteen new precatory absolutions offered by *Common Worship,* only two mention the need for true repentance and faith. *Common Worship* has also divorced the 'comfortable words' from the absolution, so that the close relationship between ministerial absolution and the ministry of the Word is now obscured.

The Visitation of the Sick

After various exhortations to repent and to be reconciled with God and neighbour, the Prayer Book service for the Visitation of the Sick continues:

> *'Here shall the sick person be moved to make a special confession of his sins, if he feel his conscience troubled with any weighty matter. After which confession, the priest shall absolve him (if he humbly and heartily desire it) after this sort.*

> Our Lord Jesus Christ, who hath left power to his Church to absolve all sinners who truly repent and believe in him, of his great mercy forgive thee thine offences. And by his authority committed to me, I absolve thee from all thy sins, in the name of the Father, and of the Son, and of the Holy Ghost. Amen.'

Let us observe some important points about this provision:

- This service is intended for use only with the sick and the dying, not with those who are physically well. Indeed, there is an expectation that the sick person will not recover – he is instructed by the minister to make a will and to put his affairs in order! Even then, this provision is meant only for exceptional circumstances (*'if ... if ...'*) and not as the norm.

- The rubric for 1549 ended with the instruction *'and the same form of absolution shall be used in all private confessions'*, but these words were struck out in 1552. Again this change demonstrates the Reformers' intentions, with the abolition of habitual private confession.

- The words of the absolution are optional – indeed, the minister need not use them at all. It is the only optional prayer in the whole of the *Book of Common Prayer*. The rubric for 1549 read *'after this form'*, but this was changed in 1552 to *'after this sort'*. In other words, the absolution is not a special formula but a general guideline. It is surprising that the Church of England has spent so much energy in recent decades arguing about these words, when considerable variation is allowed anyway.

- It is the responsibility of the minister to encourage the sick person to confess, if necessary, but the responsibility of the penitent to ask for absolution.

'I Absolve Thee'

The phrase 'I absolve thee from all thy sins' is both controversial and ambiguous. Some claim it should be understood in its medieval sense. Others think the Reformers left it in the Prayer Book by mistake! However, it is best interpreted in the light of the Reformers' other teaching. As has been seen, they did not believe ministers could literally absolve sins and understood ministerial absolution to be a

---

reassurance of forgiveness for all those who truly repent and believe the gospel. Therefore, for the sake of clarity, the Puritans at the Savoy Conference in 1661 asked for this phrase to be changed to 'I pronounce thee absolved', but the bishops refused.

There is another long-standing interpretation of these words. In the New Testament the word *aphiemi* (I forgive / absolve / remit / remove) is used in two different senses. Sometimes it refers to divine forgiveness, which God alone can bestow (e.g. Mark 2.7, 1 John 1.9) and sometimes it refers to human forgiveness, when we forgive those who have sinned against us (e.g. Matthew 18.21). There is good evidence that the Reformers intended the phrase 'I absolve thee' to be understood in this second sense in the service for the Visitation of the Sick. In other words, the phrase refers only to forgiveness of sins *against the church*, a removal of church censures and a restoration of church membership.

The form of absolution for the Visitation of the Sick is taken from the medieval Sarum rite, but with important modification. Sarum used the word *absolvo* of both God and the minister: '*Deus ... absolvat: ego te absolvo*'. But in the Prayer Book a distinction is introduced: 'Our Lord Jesus Christ ... forgive thee ... I absolve thee'. Here are the two different uses of *aphiemi*. First there is a prayer for Christ to forgive the sins of the sick person if he truly repents and believes. Next there is a declaration by the minister on behalf of the church, that the sick person's sins against the church are absolved. This interpretation is supported by the fact that immediately after the absolution the minister prays again for God to forgive the sick person: '... forasmuch as he putteth his full trust only in thy mercy, impute not unto him his former sins, but strengthen him with thy blessed Spirit ...'. This prayer makes no sense if the words 'I absolve thee' have already had the effect of bestowing divine forgiveness.

Further support is lent to this interpretation by the draft *Reformatio Legum Ecclesiasticarum*, intended by Archbishop Cranmer to replace the medieval canon law, but which never came into force because of the untimely death of King Edward VI in 1553. The *Reformatio* includes a rite for the reconciliation of an excommunicate person, in which the minister tells the sinner, 'Before this church, the government of which has been entrusted to me, I absolve you [*ego te exsolvo*] of the penalty of your transgressions and release you from the bonds of excommunication ...'. Here 'I absolve you' refers to the restoration of church membership.[24]

Against this interpretation, that a distinction between 'forgive' and 'absolve' is intended in the service for the Visitation of the Sick, it must be admitted that elsewhere the Prayer Book treats these words as synonymous. As has been seen, at Morning and Evening Prayer we read that God 'pardoneth and absolveth all them that truly repent'. Colin Buchanan, the foremost evangelical liturgist, rejects such interpretations as 'mental gymnastics'. He wisely insists that the phrase 'I absolve you' should be abolished, since it is at worst unorthodox and at best simply misleading.[25]

---

[24] 'A Form for Reconciling Excommunicates' in Gerald Bray (ed.), *Tudor Church Reform: The Henrician Canons of 1535 and the Reformatio Legum Ecclesiasticarum*, Church of England Record Society vol.8 (Woodbridge: Boydell Press, 2000), pp 488-489.
[25] Personal memorandum by Colin Buchanan to members of General Synod, October 1982.

The Ordination Service

In the Prayer Book ordination service, the bishop lays his hands on the head of each candidate and says:

> 'Receive the Holy Ghost for the office and work of a priest [i.e. presbyter] in the Church of God, now committed unto thee by the imposition of our hands. Whose sins thou dost forgive, they are forgiven; and whose sins thou dost retain, they are retained. And be thou a faithful dispenser of the Word of God, and of his holy sacraments; in the name of the Father, and of the Son, and of the Holy Ghost. Amen.'

These words from John 20.22-23 began to appear in medieval ordinals from about the twelfth century, though not in connection with the act of ordination itself. It was Cranmer who made them part of the actual formula of ordination. Some claim that these words are essential to a valid ordination, but this cannot be the case otherwise there would have been no validly ordained clergy before 1550.

Once again, we must understand this declaration in the sense in which the Reformers understood it. By using the very words of the Great Commission (as given by the Apostle John), Cranmer is indicating that the principal duty of an ordained minister is to preach the gospel. As a symbol of this office, the minister is given a Bible, with the words: 'Take thou authority to preach the Word of God ...'. There is no hint here of private confession or priestly absolution. Cranmer is showing how John 20.22-23 should be correctly understood.

The Commination Service

The Anglican Reformers revised the traditional medieval devotions of Ash Wednesday into a penitential service entitled, 'A Commination, or denouncing of God's anger and judgements against sinners'. It is a service of self-examination and corporate confession. The medieval 'sacrament of penance' was closely connected with Lent, so if there is anywhere we would expect to find it recommended in the Prayer Book, it would be here. However, private confession to a priest is not even mentioned. The service expresses hope for the restoration of the 'godly discipline' of the 'primitive church', whereby notorious sinners undertook 'open penance'.[26] Yet there is no hint of private penance. Instead the emphasis is upon direct access to God through Jesus Christ for the forgiveness of sins.

The Homily of Repentance

Outside the *Book of Common Prayer,* one or two minor Anglican documents are also offered as evidence that habitual private confession is a traditional Anglican practice. Often quoted is *An Homily of Repentance and of True Reconciliation unto God* from the second Book of Homilies (1563) which reads:

> 'if any do find themselves troubled in conscience, they may repair to their learned Curate or Pastor, or to some other godly learned man, and show the trouble and doubt of their conscience to them, that they may receive at their hand the comfortable salve of God's word ...'

This is fully consistent with the teaching of the Anglican Reformers as outlined in the Prayer Book. In exceptional circumstances, someone whose conscience is troubled over a particular issue may seek out a godly and biblically literate

---

[26] For 'open' (i.e. public) penance, see also Article XXXIII of the Thirty-Nine Articles.

person (lay or ordained) to receive assurance of forgiveness through the ministry of the Word. Again, this is more a 'consultation' than a 'confession'. The homily goes on to observe that 'auricular confession hath not its warrant of God's word' and that 'it is against the true Christian liberty, that any man should be bound to the numbering of his sins, as it hath been used heretofore in the time of blindness and ignorance.'

Canon 113 of 1604

Canon 113 of the Canons of 1604 has been part of ecclesiastical law for four centuries and was left unrepealed by the Canons of 1969. It requires a minister to keep confidential any sins confessed to him (what is known as 'the seal of the confessional'). This implies, it is claimed, that private confessions were frequently heard in the Elizabethan and Jacobean church. The Canon states:

> '... if any man confess his secret and hidden sins to the minister, for the unburdening of his conscience, and to receive spiritual consolation and ease of mind from him, we do not in any way bind the said minister by this our Constitution, but do straitly charge and admonish him that he do not at any time reveal or make known to any person whatsoever any crime or offence so committed to his trust and secrecy ...'

Once again, there is nothing here inconsistent with the teaching of the Anglican Reformers. In exceptional circumstances it may be beneficial for specific sins to be confessed to a godly minister for 'spiritual consolation and ease of mind'. Canon 113 implies no more than that.

These scattered references to confession and absolution in the *Book of Common Prayer* and elsewhere are often used as justification for the revival of habitual private confession in the Church of England. As the above survey shows, however, such a revival is out of step with the Anglican Reformers and the Anglican formularies. Although private confession is not absolutely forbidden by the Prayer Book, neither is it encouraged or recommended. There will always be some Christians who cannot find peace for their conscience in the ordinary way, however hard they try to believe the promises of God in Scripture. They attempt to lay their burden down at the foot of the cross, but somehow cannot leave it there. The Anglican Reformers agreed that in these rare circumstances private confession to a godly minister of the Word may be necessary. Yet this practice is not to be a normal habit, but an exceptional expedient. The normal habit is to be confession directly to Almighty God, with absolution directly from God through his Word applied by his Holy Spirit.

The Reformation shifted the entire centre of gravity of our penitential system. The mature teaching of the Reformers as it has come down to us in the Prayer Book can be summarised by four major changes:

What had been *obligatory* is now *voluntary*.
What had been *habitual* is now *exceptional*.
What had been to a *priest* is now to a *minister*.
What had been a *full confession of sins* is now an *unburdening of a specific concern*.

Sadly, the new *Common Worship* rite for 'The Reconciliation of a Penitent', which centres upon private confession and priestly absolution, has undone much of the work of the Anglican Reformers in this area. It reverses their vital changes to the Roman penitential system and mirrors the modern Roman rite – complete with the 'I absolve you' formula. Instead of the unburdening of a specific concern, *Common Worship* now anticipates a full confession of sins. Instead of consulting a godly minister (lay or ordained), *Common Worship* now substitutes a priest. Instead of being an exceptional circumstance, *Common Worship* now permits private confession as a habit – the new rubrics explain that the rite is for use not just 'when a person's conscience is burdened with a particular sin' but also 'as part of a regular personal discipline'. These are revisions in the wrong direction.

Chapter Five:

Is it Helpful?

It is often suggested that private confession is beneficial to spiritual growth. The practice is recommended not just for those troubled with a particular burden of guilt, but for every Christian. Anyone wanting to grow in their faith, it is said, will be aided on the journey by private confession to a priest.

Some claim, for example, that having to confess to another person brings home the reality of our sins and makes us more contrite. Yet it is the role of the Holy Spirit, through the Word of God, to 'convict the world of guilt in regard to sin and righteousness and judgment' (John 16.8). Others claim that priestly absolution brings assurance of forgiveness. Yet it is the role of the Holy Spirit, through the Word of God, to apply absolution, which we receive by faith. The words of fallible human ministers are no substitute for the infallible Word of God. Therefore, if we have a superficial view of our sins or lack assurance of forgiveness, the right response is not to go to private confession but to cry out to Almighty God for the work of his Holy Spirit and to immerse ourselves in the Scriptures.

Far from being spiritually helpful, habitual private confession is in fact spiritually harmful. It is detrimental to spiritual health. This is for a number of reasons:

- *Habitual private confession detracts from the glory of Christ Jesus.* It obscures the fact that Christ is our only saviour, mediator and advocate, through whom every believer has direct access to God. Therefore it undermines the very foundations of the Christian gospel.

- *Habitual private confession falsely glorifies the minister.* It implies he has an authority to forgive sins which he does not possess. It gives him the role of mediator between God and humanity. The minister should not be saying 'Come to me' but 'Go to Jesus'.

- *Habitual private confession is unhealthy for the penitent.* It keeps him in a state of spiritual infancy, in permanent dependence upon the minister rather than learning to depend on the promises of God in Scripture. As Richard Hooker protested: 'We labour to instruct men in such sort that every soul which is wounded with sin, may learn the way how to cure itself. They, clean contrary, would make all sores seem incurable, unless the Priest have a hand in them.'[27] Likewise W. H. Griffith Thomas once observed about private confession: 'It tends to keep the soul a spiritual invalid, debilitating the mind, weakening the moral fibre, giving crutches where there should be a Christian walk in newness and vigour of life.'[28]

- *Habitual private confession is unhealthy for the minister.* Instead of thinking about whatever is true, noble, right, pure, lovely and admirable (Philippians 4.8), it brings to his knowledge sins of which he would better be ignorant. As the Apostle Paul declares, 'it is shameful even to mention what the disobedient do in secret' (Ephesians 5.12). A minister who regularly has to hear the

---

[27] Richard Hooker, *Of the Laws of Ecclesiastical Polity*, VI. vi. 2.
[28] W. H. Griffith Thomas, *The Catholic Faith: A Manual of Instruction for Members of the Church of England* (London: Hodder & Stoughton, 1905), p 393.

secret sins of others is put in 'a place which it is not safe for any child of Adam to occupy.'[29]

---

[29] Ryle, *Knots Untied*, p 284.

Chapter Six:

A Better Way

Habitual private confession, as this study has shown, is unbiblical, un-Anglican and unhelpful. The Church of England has therefore taken a false step by offering a new rite for 'The Reconciliation of a Penitent' within *Common Worship*. Instead of resorting to private confession and priestly absolution, the Bible shows us a much better way to be reconciled with God. God's intention is for us to confess our sins directly to Jesus Christ and receive absolution directly from him – an absolution confirmed by the promises of Scripture and applied to our lives by his Holy Spirit. As the Book of Hebrews explains, Christ is our 'great high priest' and no other priest or mediator is needed. It is his role alone to hear confessions and absolve sinners. This truth is well expressed by the following two poems:

'Absolvo Te'

One Priest alone can pardon me,
Or bid me 'Go in peace';
Can breathe that word 'Absolvo te'
And make these heart-throbs cease;
My soul has heard His priestly voice;
It said, 'I bore thy sins – Rejoice.'

He showed the spear-mark in His side,
The nail-print on His palm;
Said, 'Look to Me, the Crucified!
Why tremble thus? Be calm!
All power is Mine; I set thee free;
Be not afraid – Absolvo te.'

By Him my soul is purified,
Once leprous and defiled;
Cleansed in the fountain from His side,
God sees me as a child;
No priest can heal or cleanse but He;
No other say, 'Absolvo te.'

In heaven He sits upon the throne,
My Great High Priest above;
His precious blood, and that alone,
Can sin's dark stains remove;
To Him I look on bended knee,
And hear that sweet 'Absolvo te.'[30]

'No Priest But Jesus!'

I want no priest but Jesus!
He has atonement made
For all my foul transgressions:
Each sin was on Him laid.

I want no priest but Jesus
To probe the deadly sore;
Of my sick soul's diseases,
And all my heart explore.

He searcheth, but to heal me,
His blood bedews my soul;
He speaks – my burden falleth,
He smiles – and I am whole.

---

[30] Alfred H. Burton, *A Call to Confession* (London: Carter, 1891), pp 21-22.

I prize a Christian Pastor,
A teacher sent of God,
To walk with me and guide me
Along the heav'nly road.

To lift me when I stumble,
To warn me when I stray;
To comfort when I sorrow;
To counsel all the way.

And when, the journey over,
Death's valley I draw near,
To pray beside my pillow,
My weary soul to cheer.

And, with the soothing music
Of God's own word of love,
To point my spirit upwards,
To *that* High Priest above.

No priest, no priest but Jesus!
For me on earth He died;
For me in heaven He pleadeth,
I'll own no priest beside![31]

Christ is a high priest of *almighty power*. There is no sin that he cannot pardon and no sinner he cannot absolve. Christ is a high priest of *infinite willingness* to hear confessions. He invites all who feel their guilt to come to him for relief. Christ is a high priest of *perfect knowledge*. No secrets are hidden from him; he never errs in his judgment. Christ is a high priest of *matchless tenderness*. He deals

---

[31] *Church Association Monthly Intelligencer* (October 1879), p 346 (abridged).

compassionately with even the vilest sinners.[32] What more could be needed? Why settle for second best, when God's best is on offer?

We began this booklet with a quotation from Bishop J. C. Ryle. Let us give him the last word too:

'There is nothing [priests or ministers] can do for a sinner that Christ cannot do a thousand times better. ... The man who turns away from Christ to confess his sins to ministers is like a man who chooses to live in prison when he may walk at liberty, or to starve and go in rags in the midst of riches and plenty, or to cringe for favours at the feet of a servant when he may go boldly to the Master and ask what he will. A mighty and sinless high priest is provided for him, and yet he prefers to employ the aid of mere fellow-sinners like himself! He is trying to fill his purse with rubbish when he may have fine gold for the asking. He is insisting on lighting a rush-light when he may enjoy the noonday light of God's sun!'[33]

'Where is the sense or reason of going to an earthly confessor, so long as we can have the best of all priests – the commissioned and appointed Priest, the perfect mediator between God and man, the Man Christ Jesus! When His ear is deaf, and His heart is cold; when His hand is feeble, and His power to heal is exhausted; when the treasure-house of His sympathy is empty, and His love and goodwill have become cold – then, and not till then, it will be time to turn to earthly priests and earthly confessionals. Thank God, that time is not yet come!'[34]

---

[32] Ryle, *Knots Untied*, pp 279-280.
[33] Ibid., pp 283-284.
[34] Ibid., pp 271-272.